# THE MATH PROBLEM

**Exploring the Dire Ramifications
of Compulsory Math in High School**

## THEO RHISING

Wild Remnant Publishing
Contact at: wildremnantpublishing@gmail.com

© Copyright 2025


ISBN Paperback: 978-1-997555-01-8

# TABLE OF CONTENTS

# INTRODUCTION

My wife and I have three children. After the pandemic, we decided to homeschool them—and we did so for four years. Our oldest, our son, was in public school from kindergarten through Grade 5, then homeschooled until Grade 8. But for a number of reasons—some financial, some academic, others interpersonal—we eventually decided to stop homeschooling. So, last year, our kids returned to public school.

That said, one of the main reasons we felt we could no longer continue homeschooling was math. Despite being an intelligent and capable woman, my wife often felt overwhelmed by the responsibility of teaching it—especially with three children at three different levels. And teaching ninth-grade math using the workbooks we had? That was no small task. Math quickly became a source of frustration and discouragement for her—and the kids.

Furthermore, throughout those four years, one question kept coming up again and again—especially from our two oldest children:

**"Are we even going to use this later in life?"**

It's a legitimate question. One that, as a substitute teacher in the public school system for the past three years, I've also heard frequently from students who simply don't see the point.

In fact, many education professionals—teachers, substitute teachers, assistants, and even principals—have shared with me in private conversations that they too believe much of high school math is only relevant to a small set of specialized professions. Unless you're planning to become a scientist, physicist, engineer, or a mathematician, chances are you'll rarely, if ever, need to help $Y$ find his $X$.

Case in point...

During a visit with our family doctor a few years ago, we decided to conduct an informal survey. Our doctor, a bright and capable man in his late thirties, confirmed that yes, he had to study advanced mathematics for medical school. But when we asked how often he actually uses that math in his day-to-day work, his answer was telling: *"Little, if ever."*

Despite how much the world has changed since the 1950s, the high school math curriculum has remained largely the same. Students still go through the same sequence: Pre-Algebra, Algebra I,

Geometry, Algebra II, Pre-Calculus (or Trigonometry), and Calculus. Meanwhile, society has evolved dramatically. Careers are more diverse than ever. The economy has shifted. Technology has transformed everything.

So then why hasn't the curriculum evolved?

That, in a nutshell, is the elephant in the room. Everybody knows the excessive amount of required math is pointless, yet no one takes action.

Everyone knows that much of high school math is irrelevant for the majority of students past a certain age. Which begs the question: Why is it still not only compulsory, but such a dominant part of the curriculum?

Many students complain that they aren't being taught enough about real life—things like budgeting, taxes, financial literacy, business skills, or emotional intelligence. Instead, they're spending countless hours solving complex equations they'll likely never need again.

And I've experienced the same. Despite struggling through advanced math in high school, I've rarely— if ever—used it in my adult life.

Sure, by the end of high school, most students know how to solve for $X$. But many can't balance a budget, write a compelling résumé, understand how interest works, or navigate the complexities of human relationships. After 12 to 16 years of schooling, how is that even remotely fair?

After pondering these questions for years, I've come to a personal conclusion—the very one explored in this book.

Let's not kid ourselves. The powers that be know all of this. They know that compulsory math isn't and shouldn't be for everyone. They've known for decades that public education is long overdue for a meaningful reform.

So why hasn't it happened?

What's the real reason math remains such a rigid pillar of the high school experience?

I've gone down many rabbit holes in my life. But this one is probably the most subtle—and the least discussed. As you delve into the chapters that follow, you'll begin to see how compulsory high school math may be masking a much darker agenda: one of psychological conditioning, cloaked in the guise of education for the public good.

The findings I share in this book suggest one disturbing truth: compulsory math is part of a long, gradual grooming process that begins when children are barely six years old. A process designed to manufacture obedient worker bees—docile contributors to a system that thrives on compliance rather than critical thinking.

As the late comedian George Carlin once said:

*"Governments don't want a population capable of critical thinking. They want obedient workers— people just smart enough to run the machines and just dumb enough to passively accept their situation."*

So, get ready for a deep, eye-opening dive into the hidden agenda behind compulsory math in high school. You won't need your calculator for this one— but you *will* need an open mind.

Sincerely,

*The Author*

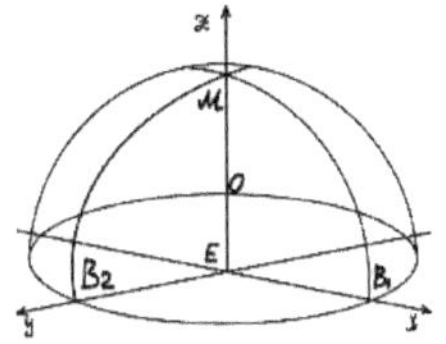

# CHAPTER 1:

# Some Stats About Math

If you are one of the millions of students who ever sat in a high school algebra or calculus class wondering, "When am I ever going to use this?"—you're not alone. This chapter is for you. Before we dive deeper into the agenda behind compulsory math education, let us begin by confronting the very practical question: how much of it do we actually use in real life?

## Everyday Math People Actually Use

For most people, math in daily life boils down to a few simple tasks:

- **Basic arithmetic**: adding, subtracting, multiplying, and dividing.
- **Percentages**: calculating tips, taxes, and discounts.

- **Fractions and ratios**: dividing bills or adjusting recipes.
- **Time management**: figuring out schedules or elapsed time.
- **Budgeting and finances**: managing income, expenses, and savings.

These are the math skills people regularly use—nothing beyond a solid elementary or early middle school level. In fact, many adults admit to struggling with math beyond that point. And they still function perfectly well in society.

**The Use of Advanced Math in the Workforce**

Let's get into the numbers.

According to a study reported by *The Atlantic*, only about **22%** of American workers say they use any math beyond fractions and percentages in their jobs. That leaves **78%** of the workforce rarely or never using high school-level math such as algebra, geometry, trigonometry, or calculus.

In another study published by the Georgetown University Center on Education and the Workforce, it was shown that less than **5%** of all jobs require higher-level math skills.

Even in prestigious and technical fields, the numbers tell an interesting story. When asked whether he uses the advanced math he had to study, one family doctor told us, "I use math every day in general ways—dosage calculations, charting, schedules—but the calculus I had to learn in university? I've never used it."

This is echoed across professions:

- Doctors mostly use arithmetic and some statistics.
- Lawyers rarely need anything beyond percentages.
- Small business owners need budgeting, price-setting, and basic accounting.
- Artists, writers, teachers, tradespeople—same story: basic math, and nothing more.

Even *engineers and physicists*, whose jobs are deeply rooted in mathematical theory, often rely on specialized software to handle complex calculations.

**Adult Numeracy: What the Data Says**

The OECD's Programme for the International Assessment of Adult Competencies (PIAAC) reveals some unsettling truths:

- Over 30% of U.S. adults scored at or below the lowest proficiency level in numeracy.
- Many cannot perform multi-step calculations or interpret simple graphs.

And yet—society hasn't crumbled. These individuals work, raise families, and contribute meaningfully to their communities. Evidently, the idea that high-level math is essential for basic functioning just doesn't hold up under scrutiny.

## Stuck in the 1950s

As stated in the introduction, high school math hasn't evolved much in over half a century. It still follows a pattern developed in the 1950s:

- Pre-Algebra
- Algebra I
- Geometry
- Algebra II
- Trigonometry
- Pre-Calculus or Calculus

Back then, society was gearing up for the Cold War. There was an urgent need to produce scientists and engineers. But now? We live in a digital, service-based economy that demands critical thinking, digital literacy, communication, creativity—and yet we continue to push abstract math onto students as if it's universally useful.

## Why the Obsession with Advanced Math?

If math beyond the basics is rarely used, why is it so *heavily emphasized* in public education?

Here's what's really going on: advanced math has become a *filter*—a gatekeeping mechanism that limits access to academic and career advancement. It's less about the content, and more about testing obedience, conformity, and endurance.

In later chapters, we'll explore how this system shapes minds to fit within a pre-approved mold— producing students who don't question the system, who measure their self-worth by arbitrary grades, and who can jump through hoops without necessarily understanding why.

But for now, let this be clear: the idea that everyone needs algebra, geometry, or calculus to thrive in life is a myth.

10/9 © 2014 Glenn and Gary McCoy/Dist. by Universal Uclick
YOU COULD GO AT ANY TIME NOW.
HA! I DID IT! I LIVED MY WHOLE LIFE WITHOUT EVER ONCE USING ALGEBRA!!
Glenn McCoy


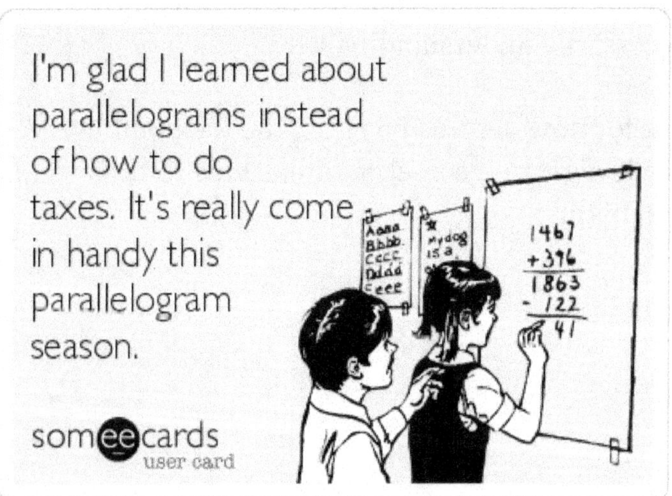

I'm glad I learned about parallelograms instead of how to do taxes. It's really come in handy this parallelogram season.
someecards
user card
1467
+ 396
1863
- 122
41

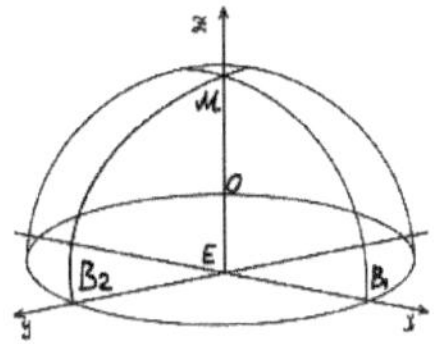

# CHAPTER 2:

# Your Brain on Math

Let's be real for a second. There's a reason why, after years of sitting through algebra, trigonometry, and geometry, most adults can barely remember how to solve for "X"—and it's not just because they forgot. It's because they never really used it. But even more interesting than that is what all that math did to their brains in the process.

Now, before I go on, let me be clear: I'm not "anti-math." Math is useful—very useful. It's a powerful tool in the right hands and in the right context. But when it becomes a compulsory grind, applied indiscriminately to every child regardless of aptitude, interest, or life goals—it starts to do more harm than good.

## School: A Left-Brain Factory

The human brain is a masterpiece of design. It has two hemispheres, often (somewhat simplistically) broken down into the left brain and the right brain. The left brain handles logic, structure, sequencing, language, and math. The right brain, on the other hand, is the creative side—emotion, intuition, spirituality, big-picture thinking, empathy, and imagination.

Guess which one gets all the love in school?

Yeah. The left.

Especially in math class, where you're rewarded for following exact steps, memorizing rules, and solving problems that have only one right answer. It's not about questioning or wondering; it's about obedience, precision, and conformity. The system isn't interested in whether you're curious about the universe or dreaming up solutions to real-life problems. It wants to know: Did you follow the formula?

But here's the kicker: when we keep pushing students to operate mainly from the left side of the brain, we stunt the development of the right. We create a generation of lopsided thinkers—people who can calculate but not connect, compute but not empathize, conform but not create.

## The Cost of a Crippled Right Brain

You want to know what lives in the right brain?

Emotional Intelligence (EQ) — the ability to understand and manage your own emotions, and to relate to others.

Social Intelligence (SQ) — This is the ability to navigate complex social environments—communicate effectively, collaborate with others, show tact, read nonverbal cues, and build meaningful relationships. It's how well you function in society.

There is even Spiritual Intelligence (SpQ) — the ability to ask deeper questions about God, purpose, meaning, and values.

Creativity, compassion, intuition, moral reasoning, and relational understanding.

Now ask yourself: how many of those are nurtured in a typical math class? Or better yet, in the average school curriculum at all?

Yeah, exactly.

When a child spends twelve years being rewarded for left-brain tasks—while their right-brain capacities are ignored or, worse, punished—they become adults who may excel at ticking boxes but struggle with emotional maturity, imagination, and inner purpose. They may become excellent cogs in the system... but terrible visionaries, weak leaders, poor communicators, and emotionally stunted human beings.

## Math as Mental Conditioning

Ever notice how math is often used as the measuring stick for intelligence in school?

A student who's a brilliant artist, or a skilled speaker, or emotionally mature—but who can't grasp algebra—is made to feel "less than." Yet the kid who can plug numbers into an equation like a calculator gets the gold star.

That's not education. That's indoctrination.

By disproportionately emphasizing the left brain, the system favors qualities that are useful for industry and bureaucracy: predictability, rule-following, repetition, and structure. Qualities that make you good at following orders. Qualities that serve the machine.

Meanwhile, the qualities that make you fully human—creativity, empathy, spiritual insight, and emotional strength—are marginalized, if not outright discouraged.

## So, What Happens Long-Term?

We get exactly what the system ordered.

A society of adults who:

- Struggle to manage their emotions and relationships.
- Follow authority without question.
- Lack inner purpose or spiritual grounding.
- Rely on external validation and standardized systems to measure their worth.
- Can't create, innovate, adapt, or see the bigger picture.
- Lack applicable wisdom and critical-thinking.

Sound familiar?

It's no accident. This isn't just bad curriculum—it's *social engineering.*

Compulsory math, as it stands, isn't just about equations and formulas. It's about priorities. It's about values. And it's about who the system wants the child to become.

The more we understand what kinds of minds are being shaped—and which ones are being ignored— the clearer it becomes: this isn't just education. It's mass programming.

And the first step to breaking the spell is asking: What are they really trying to do to our kids' minds?

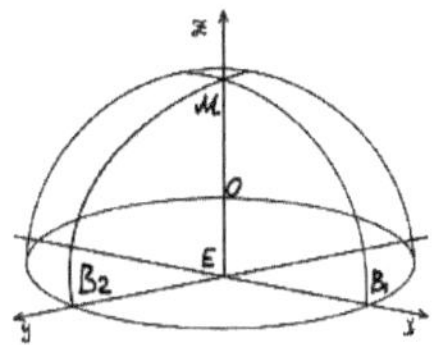

# CHAPTER 3:

# Neglected Intelligences

Here's something they don't tell you in school: There's more than one way to be smart.

But you wouldn't know that from how the system works, would you? Because for most of us growing up, "smart" looked a lot like this: straight-A student, good at math, reads fast, follows instructions, aces the test, and finishes homework on time. That kid got the praise, the awards, and the label: "gifted."

Meanwhile, the kid who couldn't sit still, who had a flair for music, who could fix engines by intuition, or who was a natural peacemaker—that kid? Often labeled "average," "unmotivated," or worse... "slow."

Why? Because they didn't fit the system's narrow definition of intelligence.

**Eight Other Ways to Be Smart**

In the 1980s, psychologist Howard Gardner came along and dropped a truth bomb that the system still hasn't fully absorbed. He proposed that humans don't have just one kind of intelligence—but at least nine.

Let me break them down quickly:

1. **Logical-Mathematical** – numbers, logic, reasoning (a.k.a. school's golden child)
2. **Linguistic** – words, reading, writing
3. **Musical** – rhythm, sound, composition
4. **Bodily-Kinesthetic** – coordination, hands-on work, physical intelligence
5. **Spatial** – visualizing, drawing, designing
6. **Interpersonal** – social intelligence, reading people
7. **Intrapersonal** – self-awareness, emotional depth
8. **Naturalistic** – nature, classification, understanding patterns in the environment
9. **Existential** – deep thinking, pondering meaning, spiritual insight

Now, how many of those get any serious attention in public education?

Two. Maybe three if you're lucky. But really, it's all about #1: Logical-Mathematical. That's the golden ticket. The rest? Treated like electives, hobbies, or distractions.

## One Intelligence to Rule Them All?

By elevating math proficiency as the highest form of intellect, the system does something subtle but powerful: it creates a meritocracy based on a rigged scale. Students are sorted, ranked, and tracked based on how well they perform in an area that, frankly, only suits a fraction of human beings.

It's like hosting a talent show and only judging the contestants on who can juggle flaming torches... while ignoring the poets, dancers, philosophers, and inventors in the room.

And then—get this—they turn around and say, "See? Some kids just have it. Others don't."

That's not meritocracy. That's intellectual favoritism.

## When the Smart Kid Is Actually Just... "System-Compatible"

Let's face it: the so-called "smart kids" were often just the ones who fit. They could memorize. They could repeat. They could sit still, follow rules, and do what was asked. They weren't necessarily more capable—they were just more compliant.

And guess what the system rewards above all else? Compliance.

Meanwhile, the kid who saw through the B.S., who asked too many questions, who needed to move or create or feel their way through life—they were punished, marginalized, and sometimes medicated.

This isn't education. This is cognitive sorting.

When a child grows up constantly being told—explicitly or subtly—that their natural intelligence doesn't count, something dies inside them.

- The musical kid starts believing they're not "academic."
- The emotionally gifted one is told they're "too sensitive."
- The spiritual seeker is told they're "spacey."
- The hands-on builder is told they're not "college material."

Can you imagine the genius we've crushed under the weight of a number line?

And worse still—many of those kids internalize the belief that they're less valuable in society. That their gifts don't matter. That they're somehow behind, when really, they're just different.

That's not just educational malpractice. That's soul damage.

## Math as a Social Divider

Now let's zoom out.

When math becomes the measuring stick for intelligence, it also becomes a tool for social sorting. We see it everywhere:

- Entrance exams
- Gifted programs
- Scholarships
- Prestigious careers
- Parental pride
- Societal status

The message is clear: math = smart = successful. Everyone else? Meh.

So, if you're a natural in another domain—too bad. You don't make the cut. You're "average," "blue-collar," "non-academic," or "creative" (said with a patronizing smile). And suddenly, your entire life trajectory changes—not because you lacked intelligence, but because the system didn't recognize your kind of brilliance.

## Reclaiming a True Definition of Intelligence

It's time to call this out.

Not just for ourselves, but for the kids who are still in it. For the young souls being measured, labeled, and streamed. For the ones being told, day after day, that they don't "have what it takes."

We need to start saying: Hey, no worries. You suck at math? No problem. You are still smart. You are gifted. You just haven't been tested in the right ways.

Because when we broaden our definition of intelligence, we unlock an entire generation of thinkers, makers, feelers, dreamers, and visionaries who were never the problem—they were the solution waiting to be seen.

# Our Education System

*"Everybody is a genius. But if you judge a fish by its ability to climb a tree, it will live its whole life believing that it is stupid."*

*- Albert Einstein*

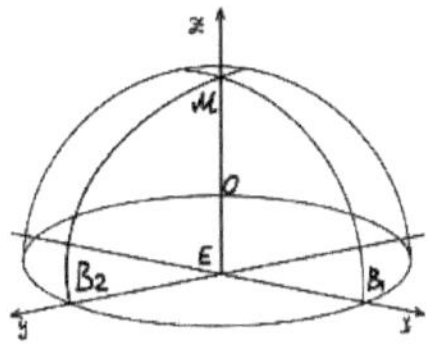

# CHAPTER 4:

# Math and The Science of Mind Control

L et's get this straight right from the jump: School isn't about learning. It's about training.

And the deeper you dig, the clearer it becomes that the most revered subject in the curriculum—math— isn't just about numbers. It's about obedience.

From the very first worksheets, kids are taught that there is always one right answer—and that your job is to find it exactly the way you were shown. Show your work. Use the right method. Don't think too far outside the box, and whatever you do—don't skip steps.

This isn't education. It's mental formatting.

Through years of repetition, students are conditioned to believe that being right matters more than being creative or original, and that mistakes are to be feared, not explored. Eventually, the fear of "getting it wrong" becomes hard-wired. They stop taking risks. They stop questioning. They become passive consumers of pre-approved solutions.

In other words: they learn to obey.

This is what I call the Obedience Equation:

Compliance + Memorization + Repetition = Approval

And approval, for most kids, is the closest thing to love they get from the system.

## Gatto's Warning

John Taylor Gatto—a former New York State Teacher of the Year who turned full-blown education whistleblower—didn't pull punches when talking about this system. He wrote powerful books that aimed to discredit modern schooling (Dumbing Us Down, Weapons of Mass Instruction, The Underground History of American Education).

He famously said:

*"The truth is that schools don't really teach anything except how to obey orders."*

This wasn't bitter hyperbole. It was a much-needed diagnosis.

Gatto saw what most of us felt but couldn't articulate: that school, especially high school, isn't preparing kids for life—it's preparing them for management. To be managed, that is.

To sit still. To raise their hand. To move when told. To think inside the pre-drawn box. To suppress their instinct and defer to authority. Sound familiar?

Gatto put it bluntly:

*"School is a twelve-year jail sentence where bad habits are the only curriculum truly learned."*

And nowhere is that "curriculum" more subtly enforced than in math class.

Because in math, the system hides behind objectivity. It tells you that math is neutral, pure, free from bias. But that's exactly the sleight of hand.

It's not about the numbers—it's about what they're used to teach.

## The Hidden Curriculum

This is Gatto's genius: he exposed what's really being taught—*the hidden curriculum.*

And part of that hidden curriculum is this: know your place.

Every test, every grade, every "honors" program versus "remedial" class is part of a silent ranking system. Math becomes the tool that divides the "smart" from the "slow," the "future leaders" from the "worker bees."

It's a sorting hat—except it doesn't send you to Gryffindor. It sends you to trade school, or community college, or straight into a system job, because you didn't score high enough on the "right answer" conveyor belt.

It's eugenics with a report card.

And again—it's not about the actual content of math. Very few adults ever use anything past basic arithmetic in real life. It's about the ritual. The sorting. The silent shaping of belief:

You are only as valuable as your performance on standardized metrics.

**One Right Way to Grow Up**

Another Gatto gem:

*"What's gotten in the way of education in the United States is a theory of social engineering that says there is ONE RIGHT WAY to proceed with growing up."*

Let that sink in.

That's exactly what math education enforces: one method, one solution, one right way. No room for wandering minds, intuitive leaps, or creative exploration. Just standardized answers on a standardized test, used to determine your standardized future.

This is what the system calls education. But it's not education. It's calibration.

The formula? Go to school, get a good job, work till you retire. And teach your children the same.

## The Drone Factory

When you teach a child, year after year, that the highest virtue is being right—and that "right" means copying the teacher's method—you don't create thinkers. You create drones.

You create young adults who feel stupid unless they're validated by a test. Who hesitate to act unless someone gives them permission. Who fear being wrong more than they fear being irrelevant. Who fear questioning what they're taught. You produce people who are conditioned to accept authority and suppress nonconformist ideas.

And in the workplace? These people make perfect employees—unquestioning, dependent on structure, allergic to disruption. They won't rebel. They won't dream too big. They won't question the system they operate in. They'll keep their head down and do what's expected.

Just like school taught them.

## Reclaiming the Mind

We have to stop pretending that compulsory high math is harmless. It's not. Not when it's used like this.

Used rightly, math can be powerful. It fosters intellectual growth, sharper logic, and imparts useful universal principles for societal improvement. But used as it is now? It's just another tool in the obedience machine.

Gatto knew this. And he walked away from a system he once served faithfully—because he saw it clearly: it's not about educating individuals. It's about manufacturing predictability.

If we want to reclaim real education—soul education—we must start by dismantling this rigged framework. That means questioning the sacred cows. That means asking why math has been placed on a pedestal. That means remembering that creativity, intuition, thinking outside the box, art, and self-awareness are not flaws to be corrected—they're vibrant evidence of life.

The system wants programmed minds.

But the world needs awakened minds. This begins with questioning the status quo.

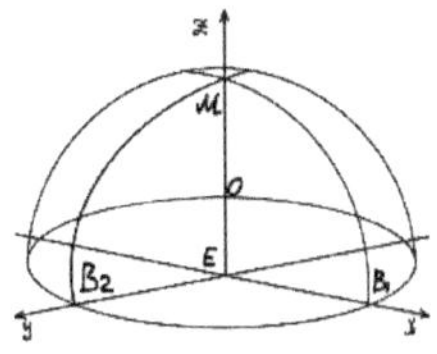

# CHAPTER 5:

# A Reptilian Curriculum?

Let's talk brain science for a minute—but don't worry, this isn't some sterile TED Talk or a neuroscientific snoozefest.

This is about how the compulsory math matrix doesn't just numb your imagination, crush your confidence, and condition you to comply—it actually rewires your nervous system in the worst way possible.

It pulls you down the evolutionary ladder and keeps you locked in what's known as the Reptilian Brain.

## Meet Your Inner Lizard

Your brain has layers. The most ancient, primal part is often referred to as the Reptilian Complex—the brainstem and basal ganglia. This is the seat of survival. It governs your instinctual responses: fight, flight, freeze, or fawn.

It's great when you're facing a tiger.

It's not so great when you're a 12-year-old being timed on your long division while a red pen of doom hovers over your shoulder.

High-stakes testing, constant performance pressure, and the shame-based grading system in math class all keep you locked in a low-level state of stress. For many students, especially the ones who "just don't get math," the class itself becomes a daily trigger. And what happens when stress takes over?

Blood flows away from the prefrontal cortex—the seat of creativity, logic, emotional regulation, and big-picture thinking—and into the lizard brain.

That's right: the more anxiety you feel, the dumber you get.

And that's no accident.

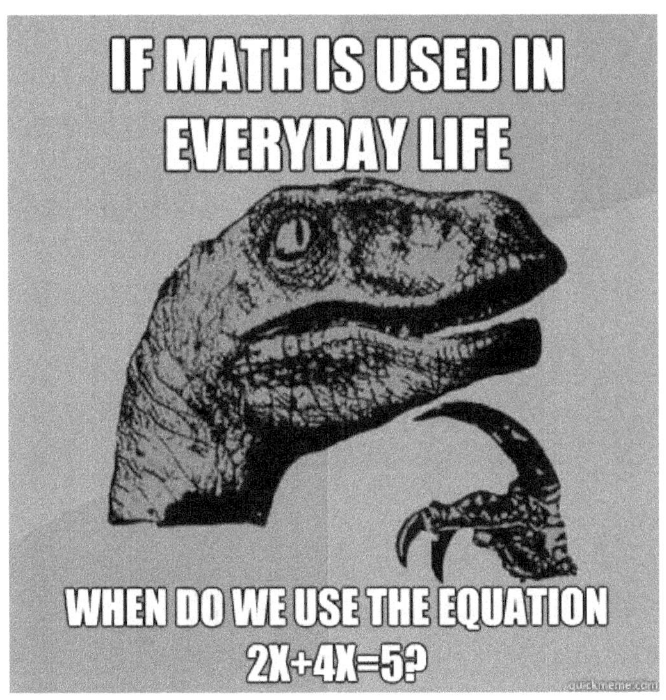


## Math Panic

Ask yourself this: Why do so many otherwise capable students suddenly feel stupid in math class? Why do kids freeze, blank out, or self-sabotage on tests?

Because the system was engineered to provoke a biological response that keeps them manageable. I call this the Math Panic Loop.

Here's how the Math Panic Loop works:

1. Unfamiliar concept introduced with little context.
2. Immediate pressure to "get it" or fall behind.
3. Fear of being wrong in front of peers.
4. Stress response kicks in—fight/flight/freeze.
5. Cognitive shutdown. Performance drops.
6. Shame reinforces belief: "I'm bad at math."
7. Repeat until obedience or resignation.

This isn't education. It's psychological warfare on the developing mind.

## Stress Makes You Small

Here's the kicker: when the Reptilian Brain is in charge, you don't evolve—you regress.

You don't grow in empathy. You don't explore complex ideas. You don't develop a sense of meaning, purpose, or connection. You just survive.

And survival mode is the perfect operating system for the obedient, rule-following worker-bee society loves to mass-produce.

While the system claims math promotes "critical thinking," what it actually promotes is critical fearing—of failing, of being judged, of not measuring up.

And in this state, you're not building intelligence—you're building emotional suppression and neural shrinkage.

You're not being empowered—you're being controlled.

## They Will Fight You

And here's where it gets even darker.

When the Reptilian Brain is the default operating system, you don't just obey—you defend the system that enslaves you.

Because that same primitive brain is also programmed to fight perceived threats.

And what's one of the biggest perceived threats to a left-brained, obedient, system-dependent individual?

You.

You—the questioner.
You—the creative.
You—the rebel who sees through the illusion and dares to point it out.

Just like Morpheus said in The Matrix:

*"You have to understand, most of these people are not ready to be unplugged. And many of them are so inured, so hopelessly dependent on the system, that they will fight to protect it."*

That's the Reptilian Brain at work. It doesn't reflect. It doesn't dialogue. It lashes out.

Why?

Because to someone locked in left-brained programming and running on survival mode, truth itself feels like danger. Truth threatens their sense of safety, structure, and social acceptance.

So, what happens?

- They lash out.
- They mock.
- They "fact-check."
- They call you crazy.
- They fight for their programming like it's sacred.

Not because they're evil—but because their mind has been colonized by a system designed to provoke defense mechanisms instead of conscious thought.

This ties into earlier chapters. Math education, especially in its rigid, test-driven form, overstimulates the left hemisphere of the brain while starving the right. The left brain is all about linear logic, sequence, analysis, and control. The right brain? Creativity, empathy, intuition, and holistic insight.

But when you activate the Reptilian Brain, you short-circuit both.

The casualty? Emotional intelligence (EQ) and spiritual intelligence (SQ)—the very things that make us wise, resilient, empathetic, and human.

And once those are offline, the individual becomes easily manipulated, predictably reactive, and spiritually sedated.

A perfect product of mass education.

## Reptiles Make Great Workers

Let's be real: a human locked in stress mode doesn't ask dangerous questions. They don't invent revolutionary ideas. They don't rebel, imagine, or create.

They obey.

And that's the point.

What better way to keep a population docile than to trap them in a cycle of chronic performance anxiety dressed up as "academic rigor"? What better way to dull human potential than to sell survival-mode thinking as "merit"?

Compulsory math isn't just about arithmetic—it's about arresting development. It's about never letting young minds graduate into full cognitive sovereignty.

It's about keeping them in their heads—but only in the narrow, anxious part.

## Unplugging the Survival Circuit

The brain is plastic. It can rewire. It can heal. But not under duress.

The first step? Dismantling the myth that math is neutral, or that stress builds character.

Because it doesn't.

It builds prisons inside the minds of individuals.

And the bars? They're made of numbers.

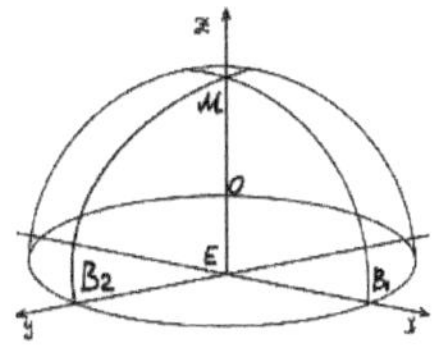

# CHAPTER 6:

# Obedient Workers vs. Entrepreneurs

Here's a question that should make you pause mid-equation:

If schools are meant to prepare kids for life... why don't they teach them how to make money?

Seriously. Why aren't kids taught how to start a business? How to generate passive income? How to manage risk, invest, or build something from scratch?

The answer isn't because it's "too complicated." It's because the system isn't designed to produce entrepreneurs. It's designed to produce obedient workers.

Let that sink in.

## 'A' Student = Approved Cog

Ever noticed how the so-called "A" students—the academic superstars, the valedictorians, the teacher's pets—are often the ones who excel at following instructions?

They're not necessarily the smartest. They're the most compliant.

- They don't question.
- They memorize.
- They get the gold star and stay inside the lines.

These are the kids who take notes like machines, ace the math exams, and master the art of regurgitating textbook information. They're rewarded not for original thought—but for mastery of the existing narrative.

And guess what? The system loves that.

Because every machine needs well-oiled parts.

And math proficiency, with its focus on right answers, sequence, and hierarchy, is one of the best training grounds for turning curious humans into obedient components of the industrial matrix.

As John Taylor Gatto once said:

*"The truth is that schools don't really teach anything except how to obey orders."*

Now contrast that with the so-called "C" students…

## 'C' Student = Creative Misfit

C students are the dreamers. The distracted doodlers. The "doesn't apply himself" types.

They're often misunderstood, misdiagnosed, or straight-up written off. But here's the truth nobody in the staff room wants to say out loud:

These are the minds that change the world.

Why?

Because they never bought into the game.

They didn't trade curiosity for conformity. They didn't sacrifice their imagination at the altar of academic metrics. They didn't tie their self-worth to a report card.

They saw through the system, even if they couldn't articulate it. They instinctively rejected the rigidity, the rules, the rote.

These are the kids who build businesses, write books, launch movements, create apps, start empires. Not because the school taught them how—but because school tried to stop them, and they pushed back.

Like Robert Kiyosaki famously said:

"A students work for C students who run the businesses."

And he's not wrong.

## Why Is Entrepreneurship Barely Taught in School?

You'd think in a society built on capitalism; schools would teach kids how to thrive in it.

You'd think there'd be classes on:

- Building online income streams
- Creating digital products
- Branding and marketing
- Freelancing your talents
- Investing in crypto or real estate
- Reading financial statements

- Building your own value in the marketplace

But nope.

Instead, kids get algebra and calculus.

They get taught how to solve for x, but never how to solve for rent.

They learn how to punch numbers into a TI-83, but not how to punch through the glass ceiling of wage slavery.

Why?

Simple... Because *entrepreneurs can't be controlled.*

- Entrepreneurs don't need permission.
- They don't wait for instructions.
- They don't cling to credentials.

And that's dangerous to a system that thrives on predictability and dependency.

An entrepreneurial mind is a free mind. And school doesn't do freedom.

## Math: The Obedience Filter

Math isn't just an academic subject. It's used as a filter. A gatekeeper. A tool for sorting students into categories: useful, average, or defective.

It rewards those who excel at convergent thinking— the ability to zero in on the "correct" answer.

But entrepreneurship? That's an entirely different animal. It demands divergent thinking—the ability to generate multiple solutions, pivot when things go sideways, and take bold, creative risks.

See the problem?

Students trained to fear being wrong are never going to take the risks required to create something new.

And that's the point.

If you want employees—people who clock in, do as told, and don't ask too many questions—you make them fear failure and worship approval.

If you want leaders—you give them the freedom to fail, fall, and figure it out.

Guess which one school trains?

The Hidden Curriculum of Obedience

From kindergarten to senior year, students are trained in learned helplessness. The system teaches them:

- Show up on time
- Sit still
- Wait your turn
- Ask permission
- Do it the way we showed you
- Follow the formula
- Don't question authority
- Don't stand out
- Don't dream too big

And if you do all that perfectly, you'll get a diploma and maybe—just maybe—a job, after you're indebted enough.

But never ownership. Never freedom. Never sovereignty.

Because that would make you dangerous to the status quo.

## A World Built by Misfits

Okay, let's name names.

Not the tech bros of Silicon Valley, not the modern faces on TV. No—the original disruptors. The ones who defied the system before there even was a system to defy.

- **Albert Einstein**: Labeled a slow learner and failed his entrance exam to a polytechnic school. School couldn't contain his imagination or his questions—so he dropped out and changed physics forever.
- **Thomas Edison**: Had only a few months of formal schooling. His teacher called him "addled" (mentally ill). His mother pulled him out and homeschooled him. Later, he would hold over 1,000 patents and invent the modern world.
- **Wright Brothers**: No college degrees. They ran a bicycle repair shop and, through self-directed learning and relentless experimentation, gave humanity wings.
- **Benjamin Franklin**: Dropped out of school at age 10. Self-taught polymath, inventor, diplomat, and Founding Father. Built a printing empire and laid the foundation for an entire nation.
- **Abraham Lincoln**: One year of formal education. Taught himself law by candlelight. Eventually became one of the most eloquent and impactful leaders in American history.

- **Dale Carnegie**: Struggled academically and had a particularly tough time with math—so much so that he was years behind and used his fingers for basic arithmetic. But he mastered the language of people. He didn't invent calculus—he taught the world how to win friends and influence others, and his books still shape business, leadership, and personal growth today.

These weren't "underachievers." They were system-rejecters.

They didn't fail school—school failed them.

And in their failure, they found freedom.

They weren't afraid to think differently.
To ask forbidden questions.
To carve their own path.

Not because they were taught to—but because they refused to be taught out of who they really were.

**The Final Grade**

So, let's wrap up this lesson:

"A" students make excellent rule-followers.

"C" students make excellent rule-breakers.

And the world changes when the rule-breakers refuse to play small.

The system doesn't reward vision. It rewards obedience.

But the future belongs to those who are bold enough to ditch the blueprint, break the algorithm, and build their own script.

Now, you might be wondering—what about the "B" students? Well, according to Kiyosaki, they often end up working for the government.

Nuff said.

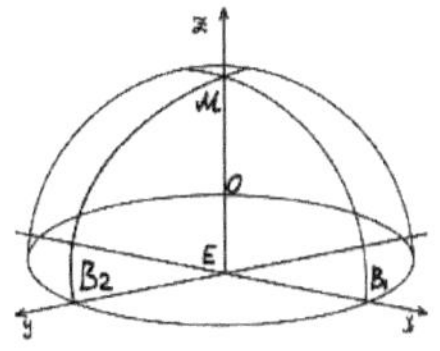

# CHAPTER 7:

# Conversations With Students

As I mentioned at the beginning of this book, I'm a substitute teacher. And while that title might sound like it's near the bottom of the educational totem pole, I've come to see it as something of a secret superpower.

Why?

Because I don't matter—at least not in the bureaucratic sense. I'm not bound by tenure, performance evaluations, or the fear of being hauled into the principal's office for coloring outside the lines. I'm expendable—and that makes me freer to address or discuss certain issues without fear of repercussion.

Unlike full-time certified teachers—who must toe the line, tick the boxes, and pretend everything's fine—

I'm afforded a rare privilege: honest conversations with both staff and students. Over the years, I've had dozens, if not hundreds, of meaningful exchanges with students of every background, personality, and IQ level.

I've come to cherish this privilege. And as an author and researcher, these conversations have become a gateway into the future. I love picking students' brains. Their candid responses give me a front-row seat to the evolving worldview of Gen Z and Gen Alpha. Thanks to them—and my own kids—I have a clear sense of what the next generation thinks about a wide range of issues.

And which conversations interest me the most?

The ones I have with the high-performing kids in high school, especially the boys who are great at math.

You know the type: sharp, quick, driven. They ace calculus while their classmates are still trying to figure out how to divide fractions. Teachers love them. Parents brag about them. They're the crown jewels of the academic system.

I enjoy talking with them—especially when the topic shifts from abstract equations to real-life applications. That's when things get interesting.

Because as I peel back the layers, I often find something deeper at play—something more unsettling.

## Worshipping at the Altar of Scientism

Let me clarify: science, in its pure form, is a noble pursuit. The scientific method, observation, discovery, testing—it's a beautiful thing when applied honestly.

But when these students say they love science and math; however, their deepest appreciation often lies beyond pure science. Often, through no fault of their own, they are led to embrace scientism—the dogmatic belief that anything not measured, graphed, or peer-reviewed into submission is either nonsense or conspiracy.

They've traded faith for formulas. Wonder for white papers. Intuition for instruction.

You want to test this assertion?

Ask them about anything outside the mainstream—alternative medicine, spirituality, metaphysics, the mysteries of consciousness—and you'll often be met with a smug smile or a flat rejection. Why? Because it's not in the textbook. The idea isn't supported on mainstream media. Because Neil deGrasse Tyson didn't say it. Because their math-trained brain sees the world through binary lenses: provable or not. And if it's not provable within the system, it must be nonsense.

That's not critical thinking. That's programming.

## You Don't Bite the Hand That Strokes Your Ego

The system rewards them. Endlessly.

- "You're smart."
- "You're gifted."
- "You're the future."
- "You're going places."

Don't get me wrong, they are—at least *potentially*. And who doesn't want to believe that? I mean, let's be honest—validation is addictive. So, in that regard, again, I can't blame them. These students are constantly being told that their ability to solve for x is a marker of their worth. Their excellence in math is often turned into a badge of intellectual superiority—worn with pride.

But here's the problem: when your identity is wrapped in a system's approval, you'll likely defend that system to the death, right? Even when it's hurting others. Even when it's broken. Even when it's wretched.

They won't question the system—because the system praises them. They will not bite the hand that feeds them. No—probably not ever.

- They'll toe the line.
- They'll memorize.
- They'll regurgitate.
- They'll get their degrees.
- And they'll call it intelligence.

Academically gifted and math-savvy students often thrive with confidence in other subjects too. They know where they fit—and they're constantly reminded of it. That's why they tend to appear more focused and have a clearer vision for their future. Ask them what they want to do in life, and they rarely hesitate. They have clarity. They have direction. They'll tell you they're going into Engineering or some other field that aligns with their mathematically inclined strengths.

'C' students, on the other hand, are often still trying to figure things out. They don't yet understand why they don't seem to fit within the system. But I always remind them: you don't have to fit in when you were born to stand out.

But the bottom line—and the sad truth—is that these math-advanced kids often regurgitate more textbook jargon and mainstream narratives per sentence than the average 'C' student. Why? Because doing so has earned them the lofty praise of the establishment.

Talk to the average student about a controversial topic—say, COVID-19, climate change, gender theory, or artificial intelligence—and you'll get a wide variety of responses. Some insightful. Some ignorant. Some honest. Some ridiculous.

But talk to a math-whiz 'A' student?

You'll hear a perfect echo of the mainstream narrative. ABC. NBC. CBC. CNN. CTV. The curriculum-approved script. Almost verbatim.

There's little nuance. No deviation. Little to no curiosity about the other side. None.

It's as if their minds have been hard-wired to recite—not reflect.

And frankly, that terrifies me more than ignorance ever could.

As the saying goes:

"It is no measure of health to be well adjusted to a profoundly sick society." ~Jiddu Krishnamurti

## Fostering Intellectual Pride?

I have also found that some (not all) of these students look down on others with a barely concealed sense of disdain. Those not taking advanced math are labeled with dismissive terms such as "weak math" or "math for the dumb." They measure their self-worth by how far ahead they are in the textbook.

It's no surprise, really. It was the same back in my day. How do I know? Because the math whizzes used to call me the "dumb kid" who took "weak math."

I once overheard a student scoff at a classmate who asked for help:

"If you can't even do trig identities, what are you even doing here?"

That wasn't an anomaly. That's the culture. And it's not coming from nowhere. It's being fed—by the system, the teachers, the test scores, and the praise.

The system, with its emphasis on math, is hard-wiring intellectual pride into our brightest minds. But their self-confidence stems not from diligent research and proper scientific method. No. It stems from following and sticking to the main narrative. All other dissident voices are wrong and should be silenced—or worse. After all, that's what the textbook says.

I still remember and shudder every time I hear the self-righteous phrase: "Trust the Science." Geez! What a train wreck that was! But I digress.

## The Bigger Picture

Now, you might be thinking: Is this *every* high-achieving math student?

Of course not!

There are those rare gems who combine logic with empathy, conviction with strong research, intelligence with humility, facts with philosophy. But these discerning individuals are not the norm.

What I'm describing is a pattern. A system-wide outcome. A mass effect of how math, as it's currently taught and rewarded, shapes not just minds, but souls.

These students may go on to become viable engineers, analysts, or scientists. But how many of them will become artists? Philosophers? Visionaries? Or better yet... rebels with a cause?

Not many.

Because those qualities require a different soil. One where imagination, risk, and spiritual inquiry are not strangled by the numbers. One where knowledge isn't just processed, but lived.

And perhaps most ironically of all—while the system hails these students as "gifted," it may be robbing them of their greatest gift:

The ability to see the system for what it is.

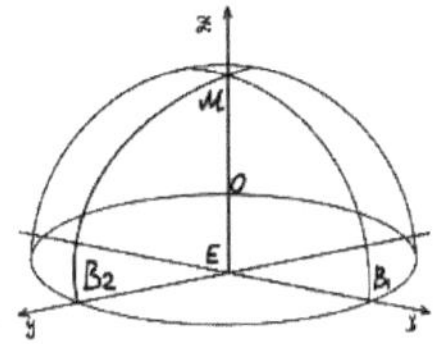

# CHAPTER 8:

# Math? There's an App for That

There was a time when mastering advanced mathematics was not only important—it was necessary. Slide rules, drafting tables, mechanical calculators: these were the tools of the brilliant minds who helped build bridges, sophisticated aeroplanes, and invent microchips. If you wanted to be an engineer, architect, or scientist, you had to live and breathe complex equations. Your brain was your calculator, and you earned every decimal point with sweat and eraser shavings.

That time has passed.

Today, we carry in our pockets more computational power than entire university labs had just a few decades ago. And unlike the clunky calculators of the past, today's tools are smart—some of them astonishingly so.

## Our Technological Reality

We now have:

- Symbolic math engines like WolframAlpha, which not only solve equations but explain them step-by-step in seconds.

- AI-powered apps like Photomath and Microsoft Math Solver, which let students snap a picture of a problem and get a detailed solution instantly.

- Coding environments like Python (with SymPy or NumPy), which automate anything from statistical analysis to calculus-level problem sets—used by scientists and researchers across the globe.

- CAD software like AutoCAD and SolidWorks, which allow designers to do advanced geometric work and structural calculations with intuitive tools—no trigonometry tables required.

- Engineering platforms like MATLAB, Mathcad, and Maple, which enable professionals to model real-world systems, simulate outcomes, and tweak designs—all without manually solving the differential equations that power them.

And now, with AI tools like ChatGPT, students can ask about any math concept—get it explained in plain English, broken down by steps, or even rewritten into code. The modern student has access to a full-time math tutor, assistant, and problem-solver—on demand, 24/7.

Let's be blunt: If a computer can do it in seconds, why are we still forcing every teenager to pretend to be one?

## Rethinking the Rationale

Defenders of compulsory math often say things like:

- "It teaches logic."
- "It builds discipline."
- "It trains the mind."

But do we really need hours of Algebra II or trigonometric identities to build character? Do logarithms instill more discipline than managing a part-time job or learning a trade? Does solving imaginary number equations create more logic than studying real-world systems, philosophy, or programming?

Let's not kid ourselves.

In truth, most students will never use the bulk of what they're forced to memorize in high school math past Grade 9. Beyond the basics—adding, subtracting, multiplication, division, some percentages, and perhaps a little geometry—very little of it applies unless you're entering a very specific career path.

And here's the kicker: even if you do enter those fields, you're not doing the math by hand. You're using the same programs we just mentioned—just at a more professional level.

## From Knowledge to Application

We're no longer in an information age. We're in the application age.

Knowing how to find an answer is no longer as important as knowing what to do with it. This doesn't mean students shouldn't understand math principles—it means they don't need to suffer through years of abstract drudgery to succeed in life.

Instead of pushing every student through the exact same mathematical meat grinder, why not give them choices?

Students interested in trades might benefit more from applied math and budgeting skills than from polynomial functions.

Aspiring creatives might thrive with design software and light physics simulations rather than matrix theory.

Future entrepreneurs might benefit more from statistics, accounting, and investment modeling than from sine wave graphs.

And for the student who does want to become an engineer or mathematician? Great. Let them choose that path. But let's stop pretending it's the right one for everyone.

## Even Experts Use Tools

Doctors now use AI to help diagnose. Pilots use autopilot systems to navigate. Engineers use simulations to avoid human error. No one is ashamed of using tools to improve outcomes.

So why do we still shame students for "not doing it by hand"?

It's not cheating. It's reality. And by resisting it, our education system is setting students up—not for success—but for irrelevance.

## A Modern Curriculum for Modern Challenges

It's time we admitted the truth: the world has changed, but our education system hasn't. We're using 20th-century methods to prepare 21st-century minds.

Advanced math should not be a required gatekeeper for graduation. It should be a specialized elective—pursued by those whose careers or passions demand it. For everyone else, understanding how to use and interpret technology-based tools is far more important.

We don't teach everyone to forge iron or build radios anymore. Why? Because times changed.

So has math.

And now... there's an app for that.

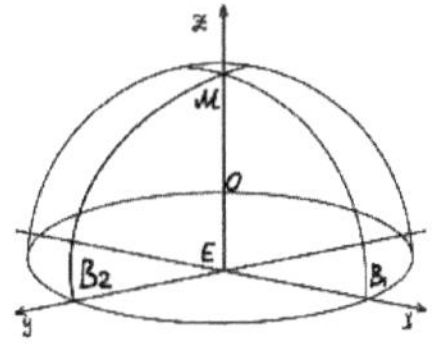

# CHAPTER 9:

# Alternatives to Compulsory Math

Let's state the obvious once more: not everyone is going to be an engineer, physicist, or software developer. And yet, modern schooling insists on dragging every teenager through the mandatory maze of algebraic gymnastics, geometric proofs, and trigonometric functions—whether it suits their future or not.

It's a kind of academic universalism: one track for all, regardless of destination.

But what if we flipped the script?

What if, after mastering the basics, students were allowed to opt in to further math education based on genuine interest and career alignment—instead of being forced through formulas that bear no relevance to their lives?

## Homeschooling as an Option

For four years, my wife and I homeschooled our children—not as a protest against math or academics, but as a way to reclaim purpose and direction in our children's learning. We didn't unschool. We didn't "let them do whatever they wanted." In fact, we followed a fairly traditional approach: we purchased quality schoolbooks with structured curriculums. There were clear expectations, workbooks, lesson plans, and yes—math.

But here's the difference: it was contextual, purposeful, and personal.

Our kids weren't learning math to pass some generic provincial exam—they were learning it to build real-life competence. They could ask why something mattered, and we could answer. They could move faster where they excelled, and take more time where needed.

So, we weren't anti-math. We were anti-pointless math.

However, not all homeschooling families use the structured model we did. Some do embrace "unschooling," where learning is led almost entirely by the child's interests and natural curiosity. Others blend classical education, Montessori methods, or online academy curriculums.

So, the beauty of homeschooling as a potential option lies in its adaptability. Whether structured or freeform, the goal is the same: to equip children for real life—not just standardized tests.

What this freedom allows is personalization—and that includes a healthier, more realistic relationship with math. In that respect, public schools might benefit from adopting some homeschooling practices.

Homeschooling proves that education doesn't need to be uniform to be effective. In fact, sometimes it's more effective precisely because it's not uniform.

We saw firsthand that when students understand why they're learning something, they engage more deeply. When they can see how math applies to their passions—whether it's music, architecture, programming, or baking—it clicks.

When students are allowed to say, "I need this," instead of, "I'm forced to do this," education becomes meaningful.

## A New Kind of Math Curriculum

Here's another radical idea: after basic numeracy is mastered (ideally by Grade 8), students should be given choices.

Some might choose the STEM path and dive into algebra, calculus, and statistics. Great. They'll need it.

Others might choose the vocational path and focus on financial literacy, trades math, and measurement. Equally great.

And still others might go the creative or entrepreneurial path, learning accounting, digital analytics, and project-based budgeting.

These paths don't need to be lesser or watered down. They just need to be relevant.

## The Fork in the Road: Self-Directed Learning

John Taylor Gatto championed the idea of self-directed learning—the radical belief that students thrive when they're given the freedom to pursue what genuinely interests them. Real education, he argued, begins with autonomy, not conformity. He wasn't wrong.

By the time a student reaches ninth grade, they've spent nearly ten years being told what to learn, how to sit, when to speak, and what to memorize. If they still don't know whether advanced math has any relevance to their life, that's not a reflection of their failure—it's a reflection of the system's.

This is precisely where public education could evolve for the better: by treating advanced math as an elective, not a requirement. Basic numeracy, arithmetic, and foundational geometry? Absolutely essential. But calculus, trigonometry, and abstract algebra? These should be options—valuable for those pursuing STEM paths, but unnecessary for everyone else.

Imagine if, by grade 9, students could choose to specialize—selecting math tracks aligned with their future goals. Those interested in trades might take applied math or financial literacy. Future coders or engineers could opt into higher-level courses. Artists, writers, entrepreneurs, and caregivers could focus on the math relevant to their world—while spending their time building the skills that actually matter for their calling.

That's not lowering standards. That's raising relevance.

## Trusting Them to Choose

The system fears that freedom. It doesn't know what to do with a student who says, "No thanks—I'm not taking trig. I'm studying business." Or, "I'd rather learn how to budget and invest than solve quadratic equations."

But those students are exactly who we need more of: motivated, focused, and awake.

Again, let's be clear: *math is not the enemy.* Irrelevant, compulsory math is. The kind that's imposed without explanation, context, or flexibility.

Let's trust parents and educators to guide students toward what actually matters.

Homeschooling, self-directed learning, and offering math as an elective aren't the only solutions, of course. But they're the ones already working, right now, for thousands of families and for some private schooling institutions, who dared to question the system and build something different—something better.

Let them choose.
Let them thrive.
Let's rebuild education from the ground up—with purpose.

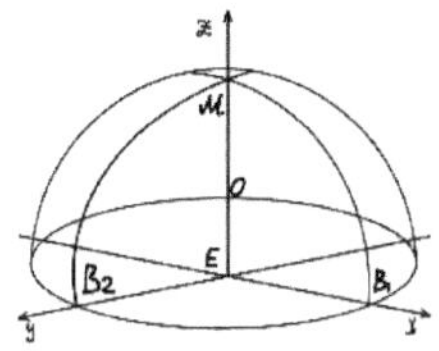

# CONCLUSION

Let's stop pretending this is about the importance of knowing math.

Because if it were about math—*real math*, the kind that builds bridges or designs rockets—we'd be offering it to the few who seek it, not forcing it on the many who don't. If it were truly about "education," we wouldn't be watching thousands of creative, capable, and curious students walk out of school every year, mentally battered by formulas that don't matter, lectures that don't land, and tests that don't measure anything that counts.

What we've uncovered in these pages is simple, unsettling, and long overdue:

As we have seen, compulsory high school math isn't just misguided—it's weaponized.

- It's a gatekeeper.

- A filter.
- A silent enforcer of hierarchy.
- A tool that rewards left-brain obedience and punishes right-brain creativity.

From the moment a child enters the school system, they're being shaped. Not just taught—but molded. Their perception of intelligence is narrowed. Their potential is boxed. Their future is stamped by scores. And for what? To sort them. To tame them. To plug them into a machine that still runs on outdated gears.

As we've seen:

- Most adults never use the math they were tormented by in high school.
- Math is sold as the universal mark of intellect, but in truth, it excludes eight other intelligences that often lead to a more fulfilled, impactful life.
- Students are trained to obey rules, not question them—a design John Taylor Gatto exposed with surgical precision.
- The pressure of math drills triggers the reptilian brain, reinforcing fear, competition, and conformity.
- Entrepreneurial misfits—the "C" students— are the ones who break out, innovate, and

build the future, while many "A" students remain shackled by their conditioning.

And no, this isn't a conspiracy theory. As you well know by now, the evidence against compulsory high school math is just too staggering. And the silent majority has remained silent far too long.

So, it's a conspiracy of inertia.

But here's the good news: cracks are showing. The veil is lifting. More parents, more students, more educators are beginning to see the system for what it is: a relic of industrial-era thinking, still churning out factory minds in a world that desperately needs artists, visionaries, builders, and healers.

At this point, reform isn't a luxury—it's a necessity. And it starts with one powerful admission:

The system is broken. Intentionally? Sure. No surprise there. Nevertheless, change is still possible if, at least, we begin to ask the forbidden questions.

- What if we let students choose their own learning paths?
- What if we taught for life, not for tests?
- What if math was a tool, not a chain?

- What if intelligence was seen as diverse, not linear?

And when I say 'we,' I mean everyone. If enough students, parents, teachers, and educators stand up to the system, this long-overdue change will inevitably come.

It's time to liberate the minds that compulsory math has tried to cage. It's time to build an education system that serves the individual—not the system or the collective. One where curiosity is king, creativity is queen, and where every student is treated not as a number on a spreadsheet...but as a soul with purpose.

And that starts now.

Not with another policy.
Not with another curriculum tweak.

But with awareness and the willingness for a thorough reform.
With the courage to say: This isn't working.
And the conviction to ask: What else is possible?

The real math we need?
It isn't algebra or trigonometry.

It's human math.

Adding Value, Vision, Purpose, Worth, Meaning.

And those equations... don't need to be forced.

They need to be lived.

# About the Author

**Theo Rhising**, a pseudonymous author, lives with his wife and three children. A man of deep faith, he has spent over two decades exploring the hidden intersections of biblical prophecy, historical enigmas, and conspiratorial agendas. Passionate about uncovering the truth behind history, spiritual mysteries and societal deceptions, Rhising tackles topics that many shy away from, shedding light on the dark corners of sociology, history, and theology.

His fascination with ancient texts, ancient enigmatic ruins, conspiracies, secret societies, and even cryptids add a unique layer to his writing, blending both faith and the unexplained. Whether unraveling eschatological puzzles or examining the evidence of

Satan's influence in the modern world, Rhising's work dares readers to question everything they've been taught and invites them to seek answers rooted in scripture and critical inquiry. It's no coincidence that his chosen pen name, Theo Rhising (theorizing), reflects his passion for exploring, questioning, and speculating about theological truths.

Through his writing, he challenges readers to think deeply, confront unsettling possibilities, and broaden their understanding of the times we live in. Living in the quiet of rural Eastern Canada, Rhising balances his investigative pursuits with his role as a devoted husband and father, continuously inspired by God, creation, reality, and the mysteries that surround us.

# ENJOYED THIS BOOK?

If so, please be kind and leave a review on: